EDEN *miniatures*

SEDARTIS

Optimist

Sedartis

First Edition

Sedartis was first published as part of *EDEN by FREI*
– a concept narrative in the here & now about the where,
the wherefore and forever at *EDENbyFREI.net*

ISBN: 978-1-64316-436-6

Optimist Books by Optimist Creations

optimistcreations.com

Sedartis

Sedartis

Sedartis appears out of nowhere and joins me on my train journey from Zürich to the unfortunately named Chur, making his presence felt in the empty seat next to mine, as I glance out of the window.

(When I say 'Zürich,' I mean a small lakeside town outside Zürich, some ten minutes along the route, where I had boarded the train, having spent the night on the other side of the hill with friends and colleagues, talking mainly about things I am only ever half sure I half understand, but which nevertheless never fail to feed my hunger for thought, invigorate my imagination and massage my malleable mind.)

Where did you suddenly come from, I want to ask him, and how is it I know your name; but before I can speak we are already in conversation:

'So,' asks Sedartis, 'wouldn't you like a boat on Lake Zürich?'

'Most certainly not,' say I in reply, though the question seems scarcely to warrant one.

'Why not?' Sedartis insists.

'Why,' retort I, 'what would I with a boat on Lake Zürich?'

'Whatever you fancy,' Sedartis enthuses: 'sail on the water, enjoy it, splash about in it a bit!'

The puppy dog wag of his voice wearies me.

'I enjoy water much as I enjoy women,' I say in measured tones, unsure of the ground I'm suddenly skating on, without consciously having made any decision to foray at all, onto ice thick or thin: 'from a distance. To look upon and marvel at their splendour, be it shallow or deep. I have no need to sail upon or splash about in them.'

Sedartis seems saddened by my lack of alacrity and produces an apple, far too symbolically. He contemplates it for many a long second and then takes a bite from it in a manner that could, though perhaps it ought not to, be described most accurately as 'hearty.'

He vaguely reminds me of a character in a book I undoubtedly once would have read, but I don't remember the book or the story (not least as I'm unsure I've even done so yet, or whether this is something I am still to do), and I feel that now he's here it would be rude of me to dismiss, blank or reject him, or to send him away;

and so part of my onward journey, simply, unassumingly and innocuously enough, he becomes.

Lesson

What, I wonder to myself in a manner
that brings to mind Morrissey, complete
with a hint of a self-pitying whine, as
I sit by another waterside—this time
the almost too picturesque, too pristine
Windermere—if life suddenly became
real? Would I recognise most of it, still?

I had not intended to involve Sedartis in
this query, but since joining me on a train
from a small town outside Zürich towards
my least favourite city in Switzerland, he
has never entirely left my side, and he has
honed to an art the disconcerting skill
of hearing my thoughts before I've had a
chance to formulate them, and responding
in kind: he never says a word, yet his
pronouncements are crystal clear.

I'm not sure I like this about Sedartis. His clarity. His straightforwardness. His unreconstructed linearity. Aren't we supposed to have moved into the Age of Diffusion? Of vulnerabilities and fluidity, of connectedness, in all directions; of openness and of infinite potentialities? I probably don't understand him, yet.

If I had a life, I would be that much happier sharing it, I surmise, almost as an afterthought, and Sedartis now latches onto me:

'Liberate yourself,' he urges, 'from the Tyranny of Opinion. Yours and other people's.'

The expression on my face betrays doubt continued.

'Banish that.'

'Really?'

'Don't banish doubt, of course,' Sedartis clarifies, as if the idea of doing so were preposterous, though he himself comes over so doubt-free: 'and make allowance for their doubting too; but banish weariness and eagerness to please. You had it once, don't you recall: the Freshness of Thought, the Arrogance of Youth, the Wonder of Everything New.'

There are a lot of capitals, all of a sudden. But I do remember, I remember it fondly and well; but was I not, I also wonder, also just blind to my own ...*Inadequacies?*

(And now italics, as well...)

'Of course you were! Therein lay your Power. Remember Goethe, remember Boldness, remember Genius.'

I do. I remember Goethe; he is, unsurprisingly, indelibly ingrained on my mind.

Sedartis, I realise, is nowhere near as mild-mannered as I believed I had reason to expect him to be. He reminds me of someone I know—not just a literary figure I have a sense I'm confusing him with, but someone I have actually met—but he's too fast for me, I get no respite from him; not at this moment, though he counsel patience:

'Learn to distinguish between those who know what they're talking about and those who just talk. Listen out for the quiet voices, the tender, the considered, thought-through ones. Those with nothing to say shout the loudest. You live in a terrible, terrible din. Find the dial and tune out the noise. Listen for the Gentle Song of Truth, it always, always plays on, it never fades out; not completely.'

I want to, I do.

'Opinion is cheap. And instant opinion may well be worthless. If you, or the person you're listening to, hasn't had time to reflect, has not expended thought, has not at least slept on their ukase then you are ill advised: heed it not. Demand earnest discourse. Reject quick fixes as you scorn fast food. You would not stuff your face with salt-fat-sugar bombs from a garish-liveried American chain. Why do you allow your brain to be poisoned by rash judgments, soundbites and rushed ratings? Insight and wisdom are dear, they are earnt. They weigh substance with value. Everything else is just froth.'

I get the feeling I'm being lectured to by Sedartis, and having never suffered being told what to do, my porcupine prickle stirs under my skin. His unvoiced tone changes. He is with me, he tells me, not against:

'Experience everything new. You once knew how to, you still know now. Free yourself from the familiar, and delve into the exhilarating fear of the unknown.'

'It's hard, that,' I offer, all too feebly, 'pulling yourself up, again and again, summoning the strength, expending the effort, over and over, from scratch...'

'Of course it is,' Sedartis asserts, laconic, then suddenly severe: 'if it were easy it too would be spume, but:...' I don't want to hear any more, I feel a little sad now and somewhat dejected. Sedartis pays no attention to my discomfort: '...the universe gives us each the challenges we need to grow.'

Autumn

'It is very nice, this very nice weather we're having:' I'm trying to work out what Sedartis thinks about simple things.

Sedartis agrees, but: 'it is also a burden.'

'How is it a burden?' I ask him, though I feel I know the answer already:

'It is also a burden because it insists on our enjoyment of it. If it were raining, or grey and drizzly, or at the very least cloudy and disagreeably damp, we would both be happiest sitting indoors and doing some work on the computer, or listening to music, or having a nap, or watching a documentary we had recorded months ago but never found the time to catch up with, or play the guitar and sing an old song, quite badly. We would be deeply content and get some of the things done that we have been meaning to do for a while. Instead, we have to sit outside and enjoy the sunshine. Or go for a walk. We go for long walks anyway, there is nothing wrong with long walks, quite the opposite, we love our long walks come rain or come shine; but with this very nice weather entangled comes an inescapable obligation: it would be a terrible waste of a beautiful day now to be locked inside and not happy.'

'It's good to be happy, though, is it not?'

'It's good to be happy,' Sedartis concurs. Yet again, I sense there's a but... 'but the effort of being happy may prove wearisome. Sometimes it is so much more agreeable to be moderately gruntled, and enjoy the undemanding misery that comes with being English in England. The stridency of happiness can be quite overbearing.'

I know he's right, though I will him to be wrong, and I close my eyes and inhale the neither warm nor cold air. The city is in constant, fuel-driven agitation: cars and lorries and aeroplanes and buses and the ambulances. Always, always the ambulances.

I like the sun on my skin and the heat that expands under my cheekbones. I enjoy enjoying the weather, burdensome though it be.

A big fat cloud starts wandering across the sun, and immediately the air feels much cooler, but not quite yet chilly. I open my eyes and see it will pass ere long.

I like autumn, though it signify decay. This year, I've chosen to stay in London rather than go away. I like London, I love London. It troubles me, right at the moment. There is too much cold money breezing in that doesn't do anything other than stifle the cracks that before let the light shine through; it deadens the life that makes London unruly, infuriating, endearing; but still I love it, because I know this siege, too, will be withstood; like the small cloud across my sun this very moment, it will pass, and ere long. I have an old-fashioned, daily rejuvenated love affair with ten million people, with more history than I know how to make sense of, and a generous, rebellious, untamed and untameable heart.

I sense there is a change in the air, and I know the change will be profound.

Sedartis nods in agreement; and with some slight tingle of anticipation, I close my eyes again and take it all in while it lasts, while it lasts...

The Sedartis Effect

Sedartis is full of little insights which are borderline annoying. They are annoying, because they are obvious, and it's possible only to be borderline annoyed with them, because they are obviously true. They are the kind of insights that make you wonder: why has nobody pointed this out to me, say, in year ten or eleven.

Since joining me, unbidden, uninvited, and taking up quasi-permanent residence by my side, he has sprung them on me at irregular intervals, which, on account of their irregularity, at least retain a mild but welcome element of surprise.

'The reason time passes faster as you get older, relentlessly, is very simple,' he informs me. I did not ask him about this, I was just looking out of the window of yet another moving train, this time to Dorset.

'I imagine it is,' I say, having for some time felt I had my own plausible theory about this.

'At the age of one, one year is a hundred percent of your lifetime. That makes it really long. So long that you can't fathom the sheer vastness of its duration: it is all of your life so far.'

I'm not sure that I can fathom it now, but for different reasons...

'By the age of ten, that same year is now only a tenth of your lifetime. In absolute terms, it may be as long as any other year, but you don't experience life in absolute terms, you experience life in relative terms, always: relative entirely to you. Your year is now just ten percent of your body of experience. By the age of fifty, one year has shrunk to a fiftieth of your lifetime: if somebody offered you a fiftieth part of a pie you'd barely think it worth eating. But it's still a year, and it's still a slice of your life. And aged a hundred, your year now hardly registers at all. You may well lose track and forget how old you are: was it a hundred and two or a hundred and three years ago now that you were born? Does it matter?'

'This all makes perfect sense to me,' I say to Sedartis, which it does, but: 'why are you telling me? Now?'

'Because you're obviously at that point in your life when your perception of time reaches a tipping point: your life expectancy nowadays isn't quite, but may soon be, about one hundred years, so around now, as you're halfway through that more-or-less century of yours, your feeling of losing your grip on time will accelerate, and because you're now no longer moving away from your birth, but towards your death, you will find this more and more disconcerting.'

'What, more disconcerting than I find it already?'

'Of course. But think not for one moment that you'd be happier if you lived longer.'

'I don't think so.'

'Because: if you were to get to the point, say, where you habitually had an active conscious lifespan of ten thousand years, it would not feel that much longer than it does now: as you'd get towards the last millennium, each year would only be between one nine and one ten thousandth of our lifetime. That is about the same as three days for you are today. You would not experience a hundred times more than you do today, you would simply stretch your living out over a period a hundred times longer. And nor should that surprise you:

when your life expectancy was thirty years or so, people did not generally think, our lives are so short; they simply did all their living inside those thirty years. No-one would argue that Alexander the Great, for example, or Mozart, didn't really get that much living done in the thirty-odd years of their lives.'

'No,' I say, thinking, a tad wistfully, of Tom Lehrer, 'that, I'm sure, no-one could argue.'

'It is, in a not entirely obvious way, not unlike the Doppler Effect: the sound waves coming towards you are compressed so they appear to your ears higher than they do once the source of the sound has passed: now the waves are getting stretched, and so the pitch seems to drop. Of course, time is no wave, and the comparison is clumsy at best and misleading at worst, but if nothing else it's another example of how your reality is shaped entirely by your experience of it. You may, if you like, refer to the phenomenon of a relative experience of time as the Sedartis Effect, I shan't hold it against you if you will.'

Counsel

'Enlightenment,' proposes Sedartis,
with troubled eyes turned toward mine,
'does not keep on its own, forever, sweet,
like honey in a jar; it needs nurture,
refreshing; the darkness around it is
strong, and it forever encroaches. Without
care, the flame will go out: the flame of
enlightenment requires our hearts, indeed,
our soul; you live in a soulless world where
your science and your money have made
you sceptical, cynical.

'You do not believe in a soul, because your
science has not found a measure or word
for it yet. Be not so hostile, my friend'—
this is the first time Sedartis addresses
me 'friend'—'to things you can't see, you
can't measure, you can't understand in
your mind: being so would be arrogance

supreme. Generations before you thought not things would ever be possible that to you are now commonplace, why would you assume that today you know everything?

'Allow time to infuse you with humility and passion in equal measure. And feed, forever, with these the light, as, if you do not, it will go out; but if you do,' his eyes now newly aflame, 'the light conquers darkness for certain, and always, just as it must.'

Projection

Sedartis holds no store with opinion:

'If you want to know the giants, the
masters, the geniuses of your age, look
whom the critics disparage. You'll find
no surer guide to greatness than them:
they dance on the ashes of the works
their alleged wit has burnt to the ground,
congratulating themselves on their
deconstruction, but from these ashes rise
the phoenices that will soar for future
generations to emulate, admire, and study.
Trust me, on this, for I know.'

What we project onto our heroes. How
we prize them; how we invest in them.
How we see our own inadequacies fade
into nothing and our misdemeanours
absolved: those sporting legends in their

own lifetime, their career years elevated to seasons of gods. Who are we then, without them. Why would we not heap fortunes upon them for the privilege of watching them chasing a ball? Why would we not conspire to see in one artist's work all our selves reflected, while in another's we discern nothing and resent being confronted with our own shadows, to the point of hatred? We are so simple, when it comes to our primaeval responses and, yes, so complex; so light, so effervescent, so intricate, so delicate and delicious, and then again at a stroke so basic. So instinctive, so brute.

I let Sedartis understand that I don't know what he's talking about.

'No matter,' he shrugs, in his calm, forever reassuring and slightly annoying because also so-sure-of-himself manner, 'it will all make sense.'

'It will?'

'It will. Liberate yourself from the urge to understand, within your head, immediately. That may seem, to you, sophisticated: it is not. Not at the level you will want to attain. Allow yourself to be subsumed into the thing around, within and through you. You will begin to sense your truths and untruths and their inbetweens in a whole different way.'

Sedartis to me seems like the philosopher from a different world who in his spare time drives a minicab in the towns I happen to visit. There is no other explanation. I would book him through an app if I had to, but he sits next to me, whenever I'm on a train. Sometimes—rarely—when I'm on a bench or at a cafe, waiting for a friend. Never when I'm having a drink. Is Sedartis only of the unadulterated mind?

What we want to see in ourselves we see in others, and vice versa. We need these icons, these exponents, these majestic figures, even though we don't know who they are. And so we make them. Of whomsoever offers themselves up. We sacrifice them to our hunger for existence: build them up, tear them down, abuse them on the way, pretend to love them, really love them. Want to be them; glad not to be them, but feeling as if we were, because we know, deep down, their existence is monstrous. How strange, and, yes, how elated.

I separate myself from my intention and begin to float. That feels lovely. Nary a care in the world. *Compos mentis* and completely lost. In that agreeable way. Sedartis smiles at me and takes his leave, for the time being only. I know he'll be back and tell me more. I just know.

Practice

Sedartis looks at me sadly. 'How is it,' he
demands to know, 'that this man is asking
for money?' I shrug, a little impatient:
'He doesn't have any and needs
some to buy food or alcohol or cigarettes
or drugs or whatever it happens to be that
he wants.'
'Yes I can see that.'

I fear this conversation is going to go
some obvious place about social injustice
and the unfair distribution of wealth and
the absence of life chances for someone
like this man, who isn't young, and who
isn't old, and who isn't distinct in any
particular way, other than perhaps that
at this moment he has just asked me for
money—for change, more precisely, which
is materially less, yet symbolically so much

more—and that I have given him some (money only, not meaningful change), partly because I for once happened to have some on me, partly because I felt unease at walking past a human being in need of some charity without offering it in the presence of Sedartis, and partly because I forever and always look at people about me who are skidding on the edge of existence and think the 'there, but for the grace of god, go I' thought, not because I have a faith or a belief or a god I can readily defer to, but because 'god' to me seems as good a shorthand for 'chance,' or 'luck,' or 'circumstance,' or 'the way the universe has momentarily aligned itself,' or any combination of these, as any.

'What I need to understand,' I get from Sedartis, 'is how do you make it so in your world that there are those who have money and keep it and then have to—reluctantly, more often than willingly—give it away, or bestow it, and there are those who do not have it, or at any rate not enough, and they have to beg for it, or steal it, or at the very least work for it; and how do you make it so in your world that purely having money makes that money increase, whereas purely not having money makes obtaining any much harder: surely, but *surely* it would be much better the other way round: what is money other than a "promise to pay," but how do you pay, if not in deed?

'You cannot pay a person in money: that is just another promise, but the longer that promise is held out and not kept, the weaker it surely becomes, not through ill will, necessarily, but through the depreciation of any hold that a thing or a person can have over anything or anyone else over time.

'So if today I promise to marry you tomorrow, and I marry you not tomorrow, and I marry you not for another day and another, and then not for a week and a month and a year and another year and another; and then five, maybe ten years pass: my promise to marry you becomes weaker and weaker, surely, not because by necessity my intention has diminished—my intention may still be lasting and good—but think of the potential lovers I meet, think of the glances I exchange; think of the buses in front of which I cross the street, think of the tall trees I walk under: the chances, the probability, of my being able to marry you ever decreases, not through wrongdoing, but because the bond between me and the words I have spoken and the thing or the person that they pertain to gets intermingled with bonds that pertain to other persons or objects, through other words that I speak or things that I do.'

Sedartis is approaching the nub of his question, I sense:

'So how is it that in your world you decree that money should increase over time: how most extraordinarily ludicrous an idea, which makes people do with money the opposite of what money is supposed to be for: money is there to circulate as an ever-weaving pattern of promises that are quickly exchanged and kept and renewed and newly directed. You give me a loaf of bread, I give you this promise that I or someone else will soon give you something in exchange for your bread that is worth as much as your bread, no less and no more, for example some honey. This can only be good and proper if the promise is called in soon. If you then stash away this promise because you know that in doing so it will become greater, then you withdraw from circulation all incentive for somebody else to garner the honey that goes with your bread. See you not this is so? Money surely, but *surely* should only ever *decline* in value over time, so that nobody has any reason to hold on to any of it, but everybody has every reason to constantly keep it in circulation, because that is all it is good for, nothing more, nothing less.'

I have no answer to this—except a tentative 'inflation?' which is easily deflected—but I try to reason, as best I can: 'Well, people, they like to save up for a rainy day, or for their retirement, say: if you didn't pay interest on savings, or if you had no return on investments, then people, when they are old, would have no pensions and no savings and would end up on the street, like our friendly young beggar just then.'

'He was not friendly, or young.'

I was trying to adopt a whimsical disposition. With Sedartis, this fails.

'Why would old people not have a pension, and why would they need savings: are you not, as a community, capable of looking after your old and your sick and your needy? Have you not developed the means to gather from each to their ability a contribution to the welfare of all?'

'We have; we have a complex system of benefits and pensions and tax credits, and then we have private pensions and health insurance and life insurance and obviously also investments and savings.'

'Do away with investments and savings,' implores Sedartis: 'they are what distort your presence today, they are the root of your immense poverty.'

'We are not that poor, as a country, for example, or as a society, we do rather well; although there are of course inequalities...'

'You are destitute. You are deprived because you lose, by and by, all sense of worth and all sense of purpose and all sense of care and all sense of freedom and all sense of joy and all sense of being.'

'But we are highly evolved, and connected; we have ever increasing levels of literacy and make rapid progress in science and medicine, and although our population is growing, we still cater for larger proportions of it better each year: we do not fare badly, though granted, perfect we're not.'

'Oh yes,' Sedartis concedes at last: 'you have the potential to be magnificent.' I am glad to hear him now thus, but: 'but you waste way too much of it way too much of the time. You do not realise your potential.'

Theory

Sedartis sits and thinks for me, slowly: 'Let me posit that there is no conspiracy.'

Where did you get your name from? I wonder. I don't ask; I know it will become apparent. He composes himself. He has sageness about him. He reads my mind, listens to it, more like; feels it.

'I went for a wander,' he thinks back to me, 'along a little lake. Little compared to the big lakes where I come from.' Where do you come from, I long to know; he stays tuned to my thoughts and replies, without words, 'the other worlds are many, while the same worlds are few. Of course you cannot know where I am from, even though you do.' I am content with that, for the time being, and so he continues:

'I do not know whether there are any conspiracies, or whether there are not, and if there are, who is within them, and who is without. There may be some; there may be many. There may be none. But let me posit that there are none: let me imagine that what looks like people consciously, actively coming together to conspire is in fact no more, and no less, than a culture.'

A culture, I think, is a conspiracy.

'Exactly. Let me posit that the conspiracy is no more—and certainly no less, which is more grave—than a culture. A culture is a conspiracy. It could be benign, it could be malicious, it is most likely something in-between; it may have, at the outset, no obvious value attached to it: but consider'—Sedartis is now thinking harder—'the good, the bad and the ugly:

are they truly, are they in themselves, are they *actually* good, bad or ugly?'

What of Mephisto, I think, less insistent than he does, is he not *"ein Teil von jener Kraft, die stets das Böse will, und stets das Gute schafft."*

'Exactly.' Sedartis understands me perfectly: he wills me to think the thought further; penetrate it deeper. I struggle. I get so easily distracted these days… 'Consider people who do terrible things: murder children. Shoot boys and men. Rape women, girls, and boys and men. Devise gas chambers. Throw youths off buildings.'

My heart feels a hollow pounding: I don't want to consider people who do terrible things; can't we consider friendly people, people who may yet be friends, though perhaps they have not met? Are we to consider the worst that people do? Why? Sedartis thinks yes, now we must.

'Consider people who do terrible things for some reason or other. Consider how in every single way they are exactly the same as you, or your neighbour, or your friend Jason, except in what they are doing at this particular time. Why do you find it so hard not to think of the other as other? Because it is exactly the same as you. The thought of it is horrendous, frightening. Of course it is true and you have to, you *have to* concede, though you don't want to, that you could be that person, you too could be doing these things, you too are them as much as they are you, you are not separate, you own their horrendousness, and they own your love, and that's what's so hard not to be destroyed by: the worst thing that a human being is capable of, *any* human being is capable of, including you; and it overshadows, for a period, in our eyes, the realisation, the hope, the belief, the truth—is it not a truth? say it is the truth—that this self-same man, that identical woman, the person who is doing the worst thing imaginable, is in the very same vein also capable of the noblest deed any human being has ever accomplished. The paradox. The infuriating, numbing, devastating realisation that the man who crushes the skull of a newborn under his boot is the same as the man who lays down his life so a stranger may live. It is not your nature to be one or the other, it is only and *only* your culture.'

But we are not victims.

'No, you are not victims, not of your culture, you are the makers of your culture; that is the call: to stand up, to be tall, to accede to the duty of generating a signal, of being a voice in the wilderness, of saying: "No. Not in my name." Of saying, "no, not in my name," when terrible acts are being committed; and of being first to hold up your hand and your head and say: "I am here, count me in," when noble deeds are done, difficult though they be. That is the choice: the choice is not between being born good or bad or potent or weak or ill or well or noble or savage, the choice is simply the culture you want to create.'

Sedartis falls silent. The thinking has quite exhausted him. I want him to stay by my side. His presence feels comforting now and serene. So much have I longed for his presence, comforting, sage and serene.

'Let me posit that there is no conspiracy,' Sedartis thinks slowly, in the way only he can, without saying the words: 'let me assert that instead there is culture. And that the culture there is is the world as it is when we're in it, and that being in it we are part of and therefore responsible for that culture.

'And when we give up our hope and say: "that's just the way it is," then we have already lost, we have failed, we have yielded in resignation to the bad things that happen, and when we throw up our hands in despair and say: "that is them, they are like this that do these things, they are other," then we have not understood who we are, not grasped that we are what we see happening around us, that we own every last bit of cruelty, just as we exult every grand act of mercy; and if we say: "they are powerful that have made the world such as it is, but I am weak," then we give away what power we have, and we empower those that we scorn for wielding their power against us; and if we think, they are evil that hold this power, we forget that we would have this power if we hadn't so feebly, so faintly, so frivolously surrendered it.

'What is power, and what is it for: it is the potency to shape the world; and what shapes the world that we happen to live in: culture. Let me posit that there is no conspiracy, there are not categories of people; that there are not those who are good and those who are bad and those who are ugly, nor are there those who are different (nor are they, for that matter, indifferent: they are simply non-different: the same); there is your human conscience, and there is the culture that you create in the world you inhabit.'

What world do you inhabit, I wonder, and think to myself, I could do with an ice cream now.

'So could I.'

Value

'The concept of "making money,"' Sedartis postulates gravely—and wonders is it largely, in character, in origin even, American, although it has now so widely, so almost universally, it appears, so comprehensively at any rate, on our little planet, been adopted—'is not only flawed,' (all concepts are flawed, he points out: it is inherent in human thinking that it cannot be flawless), 'but fundamentally, principally wrong.'

I am glad to hear this, though I can't be certain entirely why.

'Nobody makes money, even the National Bank or the Federal Reserve or the Bank of England, or any bank anywhere in the world does not "make" money, and nor does any business, nor does any person, nor does any entity ever really "make" money, unless you are thinking of the actual physical process of printing notes or minting coins, but that, as we know, is not "making money" either, that is merely manufacturing its representation; in fact, nobody "makes money," ever.'

I'm inclined to agree, and instinctively it makes sense to me what Sedartis is thinking, though I haven't thought it through myself, and I wonder if Sedartis really has, or if he's just doing so now on the hop, because he finds himself once again sitting next to me on a train.

I like the way Sedartis takes his seat next to me, mostly on trains, occasionally on a bench by a lakeside, rarely though, if ever, on planes, and never so far that I am aware of on a bus, or indeed in a cab.

'Money is not "made," it is simply invented and agreed upon in a compact between people, and then moved from one place to another, either physically (as notes and coins or cheques or other pieces of paper or some such material as may be deemed in this compact practical and acceptable) or virtually (as data), and no matter which way this happens, it is always symbolic: money is nothing other than an abstraction of "value," and that in itself makes it inherently problematic because how, pray, do you define "value" and, more to the point, how do you keep sight of your values when the abstraction of value, money, becomes so prominent in your culture that you perceive it as a "value" of and in itself?'

I have no immediate answer to this. Sedartis is not expecting me to:

'And so, not for moral or political or ethical reasons, though possibly for these also, but first and foremost for logical reasons, any economy that is predicated on the idea of "making money," and any culture that embraces this idea as of value of and in itself, is not only flawed (as any human economy always will be), but fundamentally, principally wrong.

'Whereas the moment we stop thinking of "making money," and start thinking instead of "creating value," for which, in one form or another, money may (or may not) serve as an instrument, as a lubricant, so to speak, as a convenient communication tool of quantifiable entities, such, as, and where they exist, no less and certainly no more, as soon as we do this, we can begin to aspire to wish to become able to consider ourselves an advanced society.'

I like it when Sedartis uses the first person plural as he thinks to me. It makes me feel we're in this together, somehow, though somehow I'm almost certain we're not; or rather, we most likely are, but not at the level, and not in the way, that is obvious, but in a deeper, more meaningful, more universal sense; and in that sense almost certainly we absolutely are in this together. Are we not one?...

'Creating value,' Sedartis expounds, 'is no narrow concept, it applies, of course, but not only, to making things and inventing technology and imagining art, and it equally applies to providing a service, to accomplishing a task, to building a place, or exploring a thought, in such a way that it is of some value to someone somewhere sometime, even if that value cannot necessarily at the point of its inception be recognised or defined or possibly even imagined.'

That makes sense to me and strikes me as almost stating the obvious, just a bit. Is it?

'Thus, being a good waiter is creating value much in the way that being a good cleaner is creating value, as being a good musician is creating value, as designing a good app is creating value, as singing and recording a good song is creating value.'

Who can decide, I wonder—who can determine—whether something is 'good'?

'Nobody can decide or determine, of course, what is "good," at least not in the simple, undifferentiated terms we lazily espouse. Yes, you can agree on "good practice," or define standards, but is a waiter who is slow and a little clumsy but extremely attentive and friendly and charming and perhaps a little flirtatious—just enough to send an exquisite tingle down your spine each time he tops up your glass of Prosecco—any less good a waiter than one who is super efficient but essentially dead behind the eyes and just does what he has accepted as his lot or his duty for the time being? Who can say what good writing is? Or good art. Or good music. Or good anything. Nobody can, it's almost entirely a question of taste and the prevailing consensus: the current culture.

'But what you can say, because you know when you see it and when you come across it and when you experience it—all of which is the same, I'm only emphasising the point, perhaps unnecessarily—is whether somebody does what they're doing to the best of their ability, and whether they seek to make that ability in the longer term greater, or whether what they do is perfunctory, or indeed—and that is by some margin the worst "motivation" anyone could think of—they are only doing it to "make money."

'Ask not, therefore, how you can "make money," ask how you can create value. Expect not to be valued by money, expect that the value you create is honoured.'

I'm about to interject an inconsequential and certainly not fully formed but broadly approving thought of mine own, but Sedartis is not yet done:

'Honouring value is not a narrow concept either: value can be honoured, also, but not only, in terms of money; it can be honoured in appreciation; in kind, in gratitude, in a return gesture or service, in goods, in opportunity, in experience.'

Certainly it can. That, too, though, I reckon, is hardly new…

'It is not, of course, new. It only is sometimes—too often—forgotten. Because it means by necessity that if you are doing something that does not create value but diminishes it—for example producing and selling shoddy "goods" that make people angry because they're not good and not fit for purpose, or taking advantage of somebody's situation and appropriating, quite apart from their money, more of their time, their mind, their emotion than you deserve, in return for giving them less than they need, or providing any type of "service" that does not live up to its name, let alone its promise—then you have to stop doing so immediately: you're not "making money," you're taking away value under false pretences or, perhaps innocently, feeding your incompetence off their gullibility. Either way, rather than creating value and enriching the world, you deceive yourself into believing that you can enrich yourself as you destroy value and diminish the world. You unbalance the universe. And the universe, in the long term, will not be unbalanced.'

We are nearly at our destination, I forget what it is. Sedartis seems much better now, his thoughts thus afloat, thus released, thus engendered. He inwardly smiles.

{The Silk Road}

How did I get here? To this point where, Sedartis by my side, I find myself gazing out of moving trains, over picturesque lakes, wondering 'how did I get here?' This is a change of mode, this pondering. Is it my midlife? Is this my crisis? If so, it is mild in the extreme.

Contradictions in terms. My overall state is snug, within myself. My friends, my family. I live to love not to loathe, so I tell myself, and so I feel; and so I largely, modestly, believe, I do. I anger slowly, try to forgive fast. I sense the present, now much more than I used to; I used to ache for the future, and be in it too. I may just have caught up with myself, and that is the keenest source of surprise: hello, here I am. How did I get here...

The route my father took. From Thalwil where he was working for a textile company making specialist threads and yarns, I believe (not silk, as such, it's more of a metaphor, this…), to Manchester where I was born, to Goldach where I have my first faint memories of a long balcony and Aldo our dog, to Arlesheim where I went to kindergarten, and Basel where, from Arlesheim, I commuted to school, then Münchenstein where I finished school and made friends I love to this day, to London where I'm at home.

(Or does it start with Berlin, whence my grandmother left at the age of eighteen, crossing into Switzerland and to Zürich, where she met my grandfather. That may be the preamble: there's a separate story here, and it's beautiful, but it needs to be told elsewhere.)

The question perhaps is not 'how did I get here,' the question perhaps is simply, what next: whither wilt thou, now thou art here? Not geographically speaking, of course, geography matters less and less; I am at home in London, but I can be, and be happy, almost anywhere, as long as I'm warm, have access to food now and then, and my laptop at hand with power to last, and a decent network connection.

I find myself sitting next to a beautiful woman called Karmen, spelt with a K, at a film festival in northern Italy, and she asks me what my next project is. I list four that I consider 'current.' It strikes me that this may be a lot. Then again, I have always conducted my journey along multiple tracks. Even when I decide to just concentrate on the one thing, my curious mind and my eagerness to experience tend to open up another avenue soon. I am fine with that too.

It may be that the journey that follows many roads is bound to go on many detours and therefore takes longer to reach any kind of destination, but then: what is the destination? Is there one? Ought there to be one, even, or is it not much more, as many say and everyone knows, the trip alone that truly matters.

As I talk to Karmen and tell her what I'm up to right now, and what I expect to do in the very foreseeable future, I realise that everything I have done and written and directed and made and learnt so far has been, most likely, not much more than the apprenticeship, because I sense, so I tell her, because I do, that the real task, the real challenge, the real mountain to climb and the real work, lies just ahead.

We're in the chink of an exponential curve that is about to go virtually vertical, and this means we'll not only have new stories to tell, we'll want, we'll need, whole new ways of telling these stories, and to make sense of them. 'Serious Story Telling' that counts, as my philosopher friend—not Sedartis, a friend of mine who is a real, *bona fide,* professional, academic philosopher—puts it.

I never get bored, I tell Karmen, because—as I have a feeling I've mentioned before—if you watch paint dry close up enough, it's actually riveting. But what I'm really most excited, most thrilled, most ecstatic about is that we're on the verge of understanding ourselves and how we're connected completely afresh. That the dimensions that hitherto have been considered effectively spiritual and esoteric are coming in touch with the principles of quantum mechanics, and we'll find, so I'm sure, that we can explain in scientific terms things that until less than a generation ago we thought either unfathomable or simply hokum. They will turn out to be neither.

'Look at me now and here I am,' I say to myself once again in the words of Gertrude, and I take a sip of the wine that fills me with a glow of happiness. These people, these good souls, this world that we live in, these paths that we choose or think we choose, these connections we make and that make us.

I'm in the right place, at the right time. I may not know it yet, but I sense it, for sure.

Design

Sedartis thinks we are far from doomed as a species. That, he makes me understand, is the good news. The bad news, as far as he is concerned, is that we are hopelessly inefficient. We evolve, but reluctantly so, and so slowly. He makes me feel this is my personal responsibility, and in a way it is: we have some ten, twenty, thirty thousand years of civilisation behind us, and we still allow ourselves to be stuck in our 'from zero' troubles: the wars, the bloodshed, the struggle for survival, the hunger, the despair, the fighting each other over trivial issues and slices of land, the ideological battles, the religious zeal, the blind and wilful stupidity.

The blind and wilful stupidity. That, above all, is a crime. Sedartis doesn't mince words when he thinks his essential thoughts:

'Stupidity is a crime.' Not, he hastens to add—aware and fearful in equal measure that this part of his thought may get lost, and he now forever be misunderstood—'*not,*' he emphasises, 'not the crime of the stupid. You cannot blame the people who are imprisoned in an unevolved mind for being stupid. The responsibility for allowing the perpetuation of lethal stupidity—the kind of stupidity that leads someone to speak of "deplorables," which is undiplomatic, but contains an essence of truth—lies with the educated and the informed much more than with the trapped; the leaders much more than the followers. Unless you've been given a taste for learning and an insight into what insight opens you up to, you cannot

—not unless you're exceptional—rescue yourself from stupidity. Dullness of mind begets dullness of mind, enlightenment enlightens, it has ever been thus.

'But,' Sedartis continues, with a note of concern that troubles me just as much as his observation: 'your problem is not that you don't have wisdom: you have it in spades.' I like the way he uses the word 'spades' in the context of 'wisdom.' It seems incongruous and grounded both at the same time. 'Your problem is that it reaches nowhere near far enough fast enough, and you allow the majority of your species to treat it with disdain. You grow entire generations in whom nine out of ten individuals don't ever entertain any notion of wisdom; don't even know what it means, let alone recognise it as something that might just be worth aspiring to.'

I realise this is true. And sad. Who even uses the word 'wisdom' and doesn't inwardly smirk? Have we lost, entirely, the way of the wise?...

'Your problem is that you have to keep starting from scratch. Every human born has the potential to be wise and enlightened, gentle and kind; generous, strong, humane and embracing of human nature as well as of nature itself, though evolved from the baseline of simple survival. And yet only a fraction reach their potential.

'Never even mind your developing nations, the poverty stricken and the destitute—why are they poverty stricken, still, why, after all this time, after so many centuries of science, of progress, technology, wealth, are they still destitute, *why?*—never even mind these (and they are your responsibility too), but your most advanced societies, your richest and best connected: you still allow half of their populations to get to the point only where they can barely fend for themselves; where they still feel they *have to* fend for themselves. How is such a thing possible?'

His inflexion tells me that this is no rhetorical question. It beggars belief, I know, and I wonder. Often. And I know Sedartis thinks me these thoughts in response to my puzzlement at where we are.

'Your problem is you keep having to start from scratch.' I appreciate the nuance. 'Every single individual specimen of your species is born with an empty brain. It's a beautiful thing, this potential, this clean slate, this Innocence Innate; and you think of it as inherently human, because it is.'

I believe it is. This Innocence Innate: it is inherently human. Could we love our children, if it weren't so?

'It's also incredibly inefficient.' This, I fear, may be more bad news. Sedartis thinks not, he thinks it a challenge, he wants to convince me that this is not a good thing nor is it a bad thing either, it is just a thing, and one we need to embrace:

'If you want to advance to the next level, if you want to take your next major leap, you are going to have to do something you may think of—paradoxically—as inconceivable, but that will become as normal to you as walking upright and speaking in sentences has become normal to you now: become hybrid. With your own invention, information technology. It is part of you already, you created it: far from being separate from or alien to you, it *is* you. *Augmented* intelligence. You're already augmenting your physical capability all the time, you're building body parts, you're transplanting at will, you'll be printing organs ere long. You shy away very briefly before you embrace the advantages of a body that works, and overcome any squeamishness you may have about manipulating what you were given by nature. Your next step, unless you want to stay stuck in this repetition of 'from zero' learning—which entails all your quirky, adorable failings—is to tap your brains into the network and allow new generations to start from a base above zero.'

That, I instinctively shudder, is surely wildly problematic. 'Indeed,' thinks Sedartis, 'it is. Your ethical challenges have just gone exponential. You have a task on your hands; there is no way around it, because this is as inescapable as reading glasses or pacemakers were at their time, and you've quite readily got used to them too; but this is a step of a different magnitude, and, beyond magnitude, of a different kind altogether: you will have to think about what you want your species to be. You have to actually, consciously, define what it is to be human.

'Shudder you may, and recoil for a moment, but then you have to get over yourself and grasp this nettle like all the others you've grasped, and take your people with you. Allow not half of you to be left behind and become the servants—the, dare I say, slaves—of those who push forward. Allow not your species to be torn apart into two, three tiers with some going all the way, and some being left stranded, and some unable, unwilling or unallowed to proceed, simply because they do not understand. If they understand and choose different, that is another matter. But help them at least understand. You're on the brink of a development that will set the tone for the next few hundred, maybe few thousand years of your species. Do this well: you have everything riding on it.'

Do this well...

'Absolutely.'

Sedartis seems to nod at me now. I find it disconcerting. And not in the least reassuring, not yet, not now.

"The reason you absolutely need artificial intelligence is that organic humans are so very bad at retaining information or passing it down their generations. Each newborn sets out in a quarter century just to acquire the basics, and then spends another quarter century to become a master at anything. That's with ambition. Without, you just linger. Yes, this has qualities all of its own and makes people quaint and charming, but incredibly wasteful too. The fact alone that after twenty thousand years of civilisation you still grapple with war, famine, ignorance, murder, violence, religion, all these things that we always talk about and that are so completely unnecessary, shows how inadequate human intelligence is on its own.

'But let me reiterate, for it is so fundamental: don't think of artificial intelligence as alien to you. There lies your conceptual hurdle that, sooner or later, you'll have to take: you are the intelligence you give birth to; it is not separate from you, you are it and it is you. It may yet overtake you and render you, the way you are now, obsolete, but think not of this as your failure, think of it as success: you may be no more than the conduit, the bridge. Would that matter? To you, today, maybe. To your universe, in the fullness of its time? Not a bit. So why not make the most of it? Celebrate both what you are and what you can be: let it pass through you, be the best species you can imagine. If you imagine it fully, that is not what you are today.

'If you accept that you are one among billions of conscious intelligent life forms pursuing an evolutionary path, you become both vanishingly small and insignificant, of course, but also, in the same vein and by the same definition, exquisite, privileged, amazing. Embrace your own individual uniqueness, cherish your beauty, love your capacity for kindness, and know it is but part of the All it emerged from and path to the All that it leads to. It is easy. Be not afraid.'

I detect a biblical flavour now in his thoughts and it troubles me. But I allow myself to think it is better to be open minded and troubled than to close myself off in safety, in this sense of security I know to be false. Horses are given blinkers to wear so they don't spook, but they are slaves to their riders, and may still be butchered at last. That cannot be my purpose. My task, Sedartis reminds me daily now, is surely to open my eyes. To take it all in. To be part of it all. And if it scares me. And if it puzzles, troubles, disconcerts me. And if it inspires me, overwhelms me with awe and with wonder. We are on so potent a cusp.

'I make no predictions,' Sedartis offers, as an afterthought. I know no longer what comes after, what before. What is thought, what the cluster dust of nebulas sprayed across time. But then it matters not. Of course, there can be no predictions. There can only be stories. There can be only presence, in a consciousness that beyond the boundaries lies calm across the mind.

Why, though, I wonder, is this Here here, this Now now?

Sedartis smiles at me in the way I now recognise. I like him for this, although (or because?) he provokes me:

'Why do you need a reason?'

Outrage

'Stupidity,' Sedartis thunders, 'is the enemy. Stupidity is the outrage: the crime!' Here is that word again. 'Perpetrated not by the stupid, they may never have learnt—never have had a chance to learn—not to be so; no, it's the chief crime of your society. As long as you allow stupidity not just to exist, but to flourish in your midst; as long as you cultivate, nurture, elevate and celebrate it, you deserve everything you get.'

I feel chastened; Sedartis is on a roll: 'You talk of equality. You talk of democracy and a fairer society. And yet you blind yourselves to the evil that trumps all: you lull your masses into ignorance and then keep them there. Because you're selfish, egotistical, greedy and lazy, you "give the people what they want," which you keep telling them is soft porn mush and their own supposed "reality." You invite them to be abysmally stupid on your television shows and think you're doing them a favour because they recognise themselves: you make stupidity the norm, and condemn aspiration to intellect as a pretentious frivolity. You dismiss intellect itself as an irrelevance, knowing full well that without intellect you wouldn't be here where you are, in your privileged position. You keep your people stupid because that's how you keep yourselves aloft and rich; you fear them, and you dread what they should do if ever they latched on to how you enslave them.'

There is a pause. It doesn't last. 'You feed them what scraps they already know, and shore up their prejudices; you belittle intelligence as "too clever by half"—how can you even hold on to an expression like that?—and smirk at anyone who thinks in public. How can you have built a civilisation in which not only one percent own more than half of all material wealth, but another one percent at most are really schooled in handling knowledge, when you know that knowledge is power.'

That's a crass exaggeration, and unlike Sedartis, I want to protest.

'All right, so that may be a crass exaggeration, I concede: you educate more people now, in absolute terms as well as relative, than ever before, but you've had so much time to make so much more progress than you have, you should be embarrassed that so many of you are still struggling so much.'

That, I find hard to argue with. Is knowledge power, still, though?

'Thinking,' he thinks at me, 'is an exertion, yes. That does not absolve us from it. So is walking, yet walk we must, otherwise we grow fat, stale and lethargic. Brushing is a pain, but you do it, even if reluctantly, to hold on to your teeth. Life is not convenient, no matter how successful we are at making it so. So even if it hurts: use your brain. It will shrivel, shrink and stink if you don't.'

Stink? I can tell how angry he is. 'I am not angry, my friend'—Sedartis hears me well before I speak—'I am outraged. I am outraged at the stupidity you allow on this planet. At the casual simplicity you cast over everything, and at the way you make do. At the quick quote soundbite approach you have taken to politics. The commercial current that runs through your culture. The inoffensiveness of your art. The soft sell in your science. The infantilisation of your discourse. You constantly ask: what is the simple story, what the three-act moral narrative. Because you are too torpid to connect the dots for yourselves. You open your mouths, crying, "feed me!" – You've regressed into infancy, and you wallow in your own incapacity. You suckle the nipple of light entertainment, and if you do wean yourselves off it, you go on to sugary bottled "fun," and then you wonder why your metaphorical teeth are all rotten, and you're incapable even of crunching an apple: you've become toothless, grown-up-but-refused-to-grow-up, idiot babes. You have lost sophistication, elegance and wit. You shun the strain of inquiry, and you moan and moan and moan.

'Like the whiny brat in the stroller whom you have elevated to a tiny emperor and given permission to terrorise your existence, you yourself throw your toys out of your pram and expect someone else to bend down and pick them up for you. Everything is somebody's fault. It's the government's fault. It's the neighbours' fault. It's the immigrants' fault. It's anybody else's fault but yours. Have you listened to yourselves? You are a disgrace to your species, the way you behave, and you know it, but you will stone me for saying so to your face.'

I am stunned. I have never experienced Sedartis like this. I'm a little afraid. And in awe.

He senses my discomfort, my fear. He calms down: 'Species. That in itself is too simple, too categorical. I know you need simplicity, you need categories. But look at yourselves from a distance, or look at yourselves close up: you are so near to your nearest cousins that you can barely tell yourselves apart. Yet you think you are a majestic, exclusive achievement. You are nothing of the sort, you are simply first on your planet, and alone in your solar system. But there are so many solar systems in so many galaxies, you need not fear of finding yourselves alone: this universe, as well as any other, is teeming with life.

'Your problem is not your position, not your location, not your intelligence: your problem is your perspective. Your nearest cousins, the dolphins, the bonobos, they may be a few hundred thousand years, maybe a few million years behind you on their evolutionary path, but that doesn't make them categorically different. It just makes them slower at something you can take no credit for. What you can take credit for is this: your culture. What you do with your advantage. And that is why your stupidity is unacceptable now. At one point, in the not so distant past, you were just like the great apes, scavenging for food, fighting each other for primacy over your females, thinking of nothing other than preserving, projecting, your genes. Slowly, gradually, you emerged from the dullness of your existence and you became conscious, intelligent beings.

'How dare you not use your intelligence? You will get there, of course; you will reach your next level, as every other life form reaches its own. You will merge with your inventions, you will make yourselves immortal. You will begin to populate other worlds, if nothing else as a hybrid of human and human-made machine. That is all very well. But choose how you get there. The pain that you're causing yourselves and your fellow creatures on earth is excruciating, when you already have the means to not inflict it at all. All you have to do is use your intelligence and learn that you are not the thing that matters, you are part of the thing that matters, and that is enough.'

'What is the thing that matters?' I ask Sedartis.

He remains silent. He remains silent for a long, long time, and we sit together watching the squirrels and the birds, and imagining the bonobos and the dolphins and the cows and the lions and the beautiful, but a little clumsy, giraffes.

I take his silence to mean, 'I don't know either,' and it saddens me that he doesn't know either, but I know he doesn't know either, and I wonder does anyone know, anyone in the multiverse of infinite universes at all, or are we all just a part of it, unknowing but yearning to understand, and failing but trying and playing our part.

'It doesn't matter, you see,' says Sedartis. And now I can really hear him. 'It doesn't matter at all. All that matters is that you make the most of it. Whatever it is that you can. That is all that actually matters, because you have no control over anything else.

'You can't control when you are born. To whom. Where. You can't know why. You can't dictate the terms of your existence, but you can take them and deal with them well. And by dealing with them well, you may alter them. Whatever is given, you don't have to take just as it is. What you do have to do is make the most of it. And you really have to make the most of it. You really have to not take no for an answer, you really have to probe deeper and go further and demand of yourself more. Because if you don't, somebody will. And they may not understand what you understand. But you understand what I understand, and that is how we are connected, how we are part of it all, how there is a greater scheme of things, and how our moment here is tiny, but we can, must, make it magnificent.'

Plea

There need to be nooks and crannies; there
need to be inbetweennesses.

There need to be othernesses and odd-
ones-out that defy gravity, expectation,
formula, form. The enemy of perfection
is impatience, I know, and yet I find
me a-longing, what for I know not.
Could it be as banal as attention? This
Monday was bluer than I have rhyme
for or reason. Or song. And it was the
Blue Monday, by name. Need I dramatise
myself better, spectacularise myself? Invite
preposterousness, scandal, sensation, or
noise? Or simply dress up and say: 'oi!'?

'The problem,' Sedartis muses, in what
seems a conciliatory mood, 'with standing
in the room shouting loudest just to make

yourself heard is that you don't hear anyone else in the room, let alone perceive what is happening quietly, under the din. The greatest menace and greatest wisdom have this in common: they enter the fray in silence. The menace by stealth; it creeps up on you, seemingly harmless, sometimes friendly even, or if not friendly, then maybe quaint. The wisdom though simply spreads, where it can, unspectacular, slowly, like the proverbial dawn, until it is really quite splendid and inescapably heralds the day. I'm mixing my metaphors. You get my meaning.'

I inwardly nod. None of this seems new to me, or revelatory.

'The problem with standing in the room silently, or muttering to yourself, is that you may not just be forever ignored, which is one thing, and bad enough, but taken for mentally unstable, dangerous even, certainly weird. There is nothing in itself wrong with weirdness, but when your task is to be taken seriously, it's unhelpful. Your task is to be taken seriously. Accept the challenge.'

This piques my interest: how then, I wonder at Sedartis who has been with me, dispensing his snippets of 'insight' liberally, as a Father Christmas hands sweets to children, for the last twenty months now, do I make myself heard while being able to listen, do I speak but not mutter, do I send signals, not simply make noise?

'That is easy,' Sedartis, unsurprisingly, now that I think of it, claims: 'You stand in the room, upright and tall as you are, not flustered, not blustering, not puffing yourself up, not screaming, not shouting, but saying what you have to say, with confidence, clear. When you're spoken to, listen. When you see someone in the room who isn't being paid any attention, go to them: pay attention. Give yourself a rest now and then and sit quietly in the corner to observe. There, if somebody joins you, you may yet have your most meaningful conversation.

'Keep an eye and an ear out for the people regaling themselves, roaring with laughter. More often than not they are harmless, even if they're annoying. But be alert. Keep a feeler out for the subtleties, the changes of tone in the room, the small movements, the quiet arrivals. The sudden departures.

'Listen out for the music that's setting the mood. Who do they dance to, who stand aside for. And then you may just have to pick your own moment. Because this room has no host. So it may never happen that someone who knows you invites you to say a few words and bids the others, "pray silence!" – You may have to pick your own moment and command the attention. As you are. Without fuss, but with authority, flair. Then, though, know what you're talking about. That moment may just be brief. So be prepared and worth listening to, even if just to one or two, three or four. That's enough. Be patient. Be humble. Be strong. And if you speak any truth at all, prepare to be shouted down, even chased from the building. Such, I'm afraid, is the world that you live in. Your reward may never materialise: do not expect a reward.'

I do not expect a reward, do I?

'Yes you do,' Sedartis thunders, now vehemence in his wrath. 'Rise above this need to be appreciated.' Is that even possible, I now seriously ask myself and

Sedartis in tandem: isn't being appreciated simply another expression for being loved?

Sedartis is quiet. Have I managed to shut up Sedartis? Really? I feel a minuscule pang of guilt, but triumph as well. It doesn't last long:

'George.' I don't think Sedartis has ever called me by any of my names before: 'Your need to be loved is only human. You cannot, nor should you, be super or let alone subhuman. But learn to be loved in manifold ways, unspoken, unreciprocated, unneedy, generously, unspectacularly. Appreciate love when it is not shown, not expressed, but still felt. Yours is a singular path, maybe lonely, at times: fear it not. You've been given advice on this matter before, and you will be again: heed it, it was sound. Accept love, don't crave it: give love, don't take it for granted; don't overstate it, don't desire it, don't keep it: be love.'

Phantom

The guilty look of the winner after the loser is thoroughly beaten.

'It is really simple,' Sedartis suggests, which has me a-wary, but I know him better now than really to doubt him. 'Of course it is,' I think back at him, 'but what?'

'If the young people—the generation now growing up, the fifteen, eighteen, twenty-one, twenty-five year olds, and maybe some of their allies, who, young at heart, are older in years but still see a future and want that future to be different to the present, which is, though it may not always seem so, thoroughly different from the past; and who, good of soul, and embracing of the expansion of the universe as an indication, a hint, perhaps, an invitation even, to expand with it our minds, wherever in this universe we happen to be or be from; and who therefore, by definition, by implication also, and by both conscious and subconscious intention, seek a future that is, in definably qualitative terms *better* than the present, which, even though it often may not seem so, is certainly *better* than the past, because it is wider, with therefore more scope for both meaning and interpretation, for both substance and differentiation—if young people want a future at all, they have to demand it. Not ask for it nicely, not politely sit in the corner waiting for it to be offered, not wonder will it be offered at all, but get out on the street, get up on the box, get into the fray, whatever, wherever it may be, literally, metaphorically, passionately, and demand it, their future.

'Because the old people will mess it up for them, for certain. There is no alternative, sadly, and no alternative outcome, because old people—with comparatively few and notable, also respectable, exceptions—are inclined (I'm inclined to say "programmed") to maintain their status quo, for no other reason than that it is familiar, comfortable.

'But realise, of course, that in an expanding universe there is no standing still. If you cling on to the status quo, thinking it stable, thinking it solid, thinking it, therefore, by definition and by implication, dependable and so, if nothing else, for yourself, "good," you are in fact regressing. In a world like yours in which—as in all worlds currently known to anyone—entropy is an inescapable principle at work on everything, stagnation is a move to obsolescence. Old people—always allowing for significant, but comparatively small, numbers of exceptions—surrender to their own fate of obsolescence long before they reach it, and that is why old people cannot, in their majority, help but mess things up for the young.

So unless young people get up and demand their future, there can be none. There can only be the status quo, which is in fact a regression, which is the past. Which is definitely and infinitely worse than the future. It has to be, because this whole universe was smaller, narrower, more confined than it is now and than it will be, with therefore less room, both literally and metaphorically, and less time, both literally and metaphorically, in it to think, and invent, to love, and to be.

'How mundane it seems to me, as you can imagine, to cite for you concrete examples, but since you ask'—I didn't think I was asking—'take the obvious ones, the ones in your "news" right now, as we converse: If young people are in Britain and want a future in Europe they have to demand it. If they are in the United States and they want to survive their school years, they have to demand it. Demand freedom of movement. Demand education in unarmed environments. Demand the right to live somewhere affordable, clean, safe and sane. Demand free and comprehensive health care. Demand the right to speak and think freely, and to disagree with anything I, or you, or anybody else is saying. That's the promise of civilisation, everything else is barbaric.

'Your youth has to claim civilisation. Not with violence, of course, but with power. Their force is in their numbers and in their energy, in their ingenuity and in their spirit. Their force is their future. They must use it. You can't do it for them. But,' and here Sedartis changes his tone, and, for the first time ever, I hear him sound almost seductive, 'you can help them: you can tell them you are on their side, you can let them know you want their future for them as much as they do, and they will understand; because of course they know all this already, they don't need to be told, they just—if anything—need to be encouraged. Reassured maybe. To know that you don't hold their rebellion against your present as directed against you, but only against your present, and that their demand, no matter how unreasonable it may be made to sound by those who oppose it, is reasonable, essential even, to the continuation of your civilisation. They instinctively know this. They need, if anything, only perhaps to be reminded.

'Remind them only: you are on their side. You want them to live and to thrive. You want them to stand up for their future. Because if they don't, their misery will be great, and their death, their despair, their destruction long. And it will fall to their miserable, angry children to do what their parents failed to do: to demand—not request, not beg, not buy and not steal—to demand and so shape their own future.'

Critical Mass

'What if,' Sedartis muses, 'consciousness is not a matter of characteristics or substance or physics or chemistry or biology or the nature of the configuration of brain cells or the genetic make-up or the design, divine or otherwise, of the brain or its configuration with the rest of the body, but merely a matter of connective concentration: get enough nodes on the network—in your case, the brain—to connect with each other at high enough speed and frequency, and you reach the point at which the network—in your case still the brain—becomes aware of itself and can start making decisions that are self-conscious.

'Apply that principle to any other network capable of processing information—

computers, chips, civilisations, planets with technological infrastructure and already conscious entities on them—and you enter the exponential acceleration of intelligence. Why? Precisely because it is networked to the level where it can become conscious. What if Consciousness is nothing but this: enough capable nodes on the network, Critical Mass.'

I'm inclined, unsurprisingly, to consider that a real possibility...

www.ingramcontent.com/pod-product-compliance
Ingram Content Group UK Ltd.
Pitfield, Milton Keynes, MK11 3LW, UK
UKHW041842200726
13854UKWH00005BA/1988
9 781643 164366